Bread sculptures techniques

Bread sculptures

van Dobbenburgh Amsterdam/Kidderminster

Original titel. Brooddeeg technieken
Editor: Helmke van Geel
Translation from the Dutch
The Old Rectory, Pyworthy,
Holsworthy, Devon. Ex 22 6LA, England

Copyright © 1985
Uitgeverij van Dobbenburgh b.v., Amsterdam Holland./

English Edition distributed by
Ruskin Book services Ltd.
15 Comberton Hill, Kidderminster
Worcestershire DY 10 1QG U.K.
Telephone 0562 515151 and 68014
Telex RBS 335672
Printed in Spain by I.G. Domingo, S.A. San Joan Despí

ISBN 9-06-577034-8

Contents

Bread dough through the ages up to the present day

In all ancient cultures bread played an important part in the daily life of man, and it has continued to do so for centuries. Archaeological discoveries have shown that our ancestors were baking bread in the form of flat loaves some 8,000 years ago. Bread became an important part of the staple diet but it was also more than that. Because of the central role played by bread in life, it also acquired a deeper significance. Gradually rituals evolved around the grain, the corn, the sowing, harvesting and kneading and baking of the bread itself, and we can no longer imagine being without these. The discovery of the conserving properties of salt probably first gave man the idea of baking bread for purposes other than consumption.

People found ways of expressing their ideas and feelings through their bread. Though it may sound far-fetched, it would be quite possible to write a history of human culture based on these two aspects of bread – as a source of food and as a means of expression.

Particularly in those cultures in which bread formed the staple diet, bread was identified with nature, fertility and divine mystery. Dough was an inexhaustible source of inspiration for baking all sorts of remarkable figures in ancient times, which were then offered as gifts to the gods, as a way of showing man's gratitude for divine protection. At first the offerings were simple round loaves, but gradually these developed and began to represent beautiful figures and scenes.

There are some good examples of these from the Greek, and later from the Roman civilisation. Bread was also considered a holy sacrament in the Christian culture, for example, in the form of the consecrated host which is taken by Catholics at communion. This sacred character of bread also led to other uses, for example, beautifully formed garlands are still offered to the Virgin Mary in the Spanish village of Llanes to this very day.

In addition, bread figures were baked as symbols of fertility in a number of different cultures. For example, in India bread figures are used as lucky talismans for the following harvest, while the richly decorated garlands of bread dough were offered as presents at a marriage feast on the island of Crete.

In Mexico figures made of bread dough played an important part in the ritual surrounding the worship of the dead. The beautifully painted trees of life which were buried with the dead in the hope of securing their immortality, are famous.

This centuries-old tradition of baking bread for special occasions or religious rituals is still very common nowadays in a number of countries. At Easter and Christmas, bakers in the Netherlands still vie to see who can bake the most beautiful loaves or bread figures. In addition, this ancient popular art form has been rediscovered by 20th century man as an extremely pleasant and decorative hobby. The ingredients and materials required for the dough are cheap, and the dough itself is very easy to make. Yet there is a wealth of creative possibilities in this dough.

By adding glycerine (wallpaper paste) you can turn the bread dough into a firm modelling clay which is almost comparable to the best type of clay available.

A whole world of possibilities lies before you – from making the most splendid wall decorations to very original presents and even individual works of art.

This book will help you on your way in this art form. It begins with a short survey of the most important facts and a number of practical tips.

This is followed by descriptions of how to

make a number of figures, accompanied by a series of extremely clear photographs. All the pieces which are photographed were made by people who do bread sculpture as a hobby, and not by professionals.

This should serve to assure you that the figures in our examples can be made with straightforward materials by anyone who is enthusiastic about this art form. Obviously this book does not aim to provide an exhaustive list of models and figures because eventually the intention is that you will come up with your own ideas and variations. If you have never done any bread sculpture before, it is undoubtedly best to begin with some simple examples. You will soon find that you gradually acquire the art of modelling the dough and that you are ready to venture onto larger and more complicated projects. We wish you all the best in your endeavours.

Making an entire tableau always produces a great sense of satisfaction. The tableau shown here is based on an original design and incorporates all sorts of materials such as small pebbles, cloves, berries, pieces of string, and a wooden stick.

The bread figures which appear in this book were made by:

Ini Bakker
Pps. 17, 54, 55, 56, 57, 58, 64, 65, 66, 67, 68, 69, 70, 71, 93 bottom right and 94 top right.

Etty Hendrikse-Posthuma
Pps. 60, 61, 62, 63, 72, 73, 74, 75, 76, 77, 78, 79, 80, 81, 82, 83, 84, 85, 87, 88, 89, 90, 93

Ike Schotanus
Pps. 24, 25, 26, 27, 28, 29, 30, 31, 32, 33, 34, 35, 36, 37, 38, 39, 40, 41, 42, 43, 44, 45, 46, 47, 93, left and top right

Christine Sluis
Pps. 10, 18, 20, 21, 22, 23, 50, 51, 52, 53, 93, bottom left and 94, top left.

Tekst KLUB, Weesp

Tools and materials

Tools
- bowl
- whisk
- work surface, wooden board, piece of hard plastic (to provide a good base for kneading and modelling)
- rolling pin (for rolling out flat pieces of dough)
- garlic press (to press thin strands of dough)
- fish slice or pancake slice (for lifting and moving the figures)
- sharp knife (for cutting shapes)
- modelling spatulas
- pattern cutters, glasses etc. for cutting shapes
- skewers, nails, screws, plugs, needles, cocktail sticks, buttons, straws etc. (for working and decorating the dough figures)
- a pair of compasses (for drawing the base)
- various brushes (for applying varnish or water)

Materials
- flour (*not* self-raising flour)
- water
- glycerine (wallpaper paste)
- varnish or yacht varnish
- acrylic paint, poster paint, batik dye
- natural dyes such as coffee, cocoa and cinnamon
- aluminium foil (as a background for the figures while you are modelling and baking)
- decorations such as dried flowers, beads, marbles, buttons, ribbons etc.

Preparing the dough

The dry ingredients, flour, salt and glycerine should first be mixed thoroughly in a large bowl. The reason why self-raising flour should certainly not be used is self evident: if the bread figures rise in the oven, they may change shape in an unacceptable manner. A cup of water is then added to this dry mixture, stirring constantly with a whisk so that the flour does not go lumpy.

Very fine dough, suitable for small, complicated figures, can be obtained by first dissolving the salt in the water and mixing the mixture with an electric mixer for about five minutes. Then add this to the flour and glycerine whilst stirring constantly.

When the mixture in the bowl has gone fairly stiff, you can take it out of the bowl and knead it.

You should knead the dough for at least ten minutes on a flat surface, e.g., a wooden board or formica work top.

If the dough is still sticky, add a small amount of flour; sometimes merely rolling the dough in the flour will be sufficient. On the other hand, if the dough feels too dry, it can be lightly sprayed with water or brushed with a wet brush.

Another solution might be to knead the dough with wet hands.

The dough may also be too dry or too sticky as a result of the temperature in the room where you are working. High temperatures will result in thin, sticky dough (add a little flour) and low temperatures will lead to rather hard and crumbly dough (add a little bit of warm water).

Kneading the dough for a long time will make it increasingly flexible and airy. Remember that this dough can later be used to make any figure you wish, and if you have kneaded the dough thoroughly, you will reap the benefit later. Supple and slightly moist dough is particularly important for small, detailed figures. The small amount of glycerine added earlier will help as it firms the dough up and in addition, makes it possible to stick the separate parts of a larger composition together as a sort of glue.

Long, thorough kneading is one of the most important prerequisites of satisfactory dough – so don't stop kneading too soon.

Storing the dough

If you do not need to use all the dough you have prepared immediately, it is possible to keep the remainder in a plastic bag or bowl for a few days.

It is possible that the dough may become too moist after it has been kept for a few days. This problem can easily be solved by again rolling it lightly through the flour and kneading it.

Recipe

3 cups of flour
(use plain flour,
never self-raising flour)

1 cup of salt
(fine grained kitchen salt)

1 cup of water

1 teaspoon of glycerine
(wallpaper paste)

Coloured dough

If you wish to give the dough a different colour from the natural shade of light brown, there are various different ways of doing this. Dyeing the dough in advance can produce beautiful colours and in addition saves a lot of work painting the figure after it has been baked.

Cocoa, coffee and cinnamon
First, there is the possibility of colouring the dough with natural dyes such as coffee, cocoa and cinnamon.
You add these ingredients to a cup of water and then pour the mixture into a small pan to bring it to the boil. When the coffee, cocoa and cinnamon have been satisfactorily dissolved, stirring constantly with a wooden whisk, leave the mixture to cool thoroughly before adding it to the flour, the salt and the glycerine.

Batik dye
Another method of colouring the dough in advance that can be used to achieve many different effects, is to use batik dyes. You will find batik dyes in many beautiful pastel shades in any good shop selling artists' materials.
When you use batik dyes, follow the procedure outlined above. First dissolve the dye in the water, then heat it to boiling point, leave to cool thoroughly and then add to the other ingredients.

Wholemeal or rye flour
A very easy way of making your figures a slightly darker brown colour is simply to replace the plain flour with wholemeal or rye flour. If you use wholemeal or rye flour on their own, this will result in a deep brown colour after baking.
Obviously it is always possible to obtain countless intermediate shades of brown by mixing the rye or wholemeal flour with ordinary white flour in advance, in the required proportions.

A two-tone sheep; the fleece is made from dough to which some cocoa has been added. Paint has only been used to emphasize the eyes.

A good start

Do not simply start on your bread sculpture as soon as you have made the dough without making any preparations. Remember to check the following points:

— First collect together all the tools and materials you require and then put them ready on the work surface so that you know where they are and they are at hand as soon as you need them. Also make sure that there is some space left on the work surface where you can roll out and cut out the bases for your figures.

— It is best to model and work on the figures with a piece of aluminium foil as a base. Aluminium foil does not stick to the dough, and in addition this will make it easier to move the figures. It is even possible to put the figures in the oven with the aluminium foil to minimise the chance of damage.

— Always make sure you have a bowl of clean water and a brush handy. Small, loose parts of your dough figure will soon dry out (particularly in a warm work area) so that they can no longer be used. If necessary, brush the figures regularly with a little water. If the room is on the cold side, it is a good idea to use slightly warm water.
You will also need a bowl of water and a brush for joining the separate pieces together. This 'gluing' is easier when the dough is slightly moist.

— Before starting on your figure it is essential to decide on the basic shape and make a rough sketch.
Once you have finished the basic shape of the frame you can let your imagination loose on the details which will complete the figure.

Baking

Obviously an extremely important part of bread sculpture is the baking process. If the figures are baked carefully this will ensure that your creations will keep so that you can enjoy them for a long time.

Preparation
If you wish to reduce the baking time this can be done by leaving the figure to dry out first. However, if you leave it to dry in the open air, there is a danger that the surface will go hard and crusty.
This means that the surface does not allow air to pass through so that the dough inside remains moist. This can give rise to tension leading to cracks or changes in shape in the figure. Obviously this does not apply to the same extent to thin, flat figures.
If you decide to let the figures dry out in advance, it is advisable to find a dry, warm place for this. They should be placed on dry newspaper and turned over from time to time.
When you are ready to bake the figure, place it on a lightly greased baking tray or, more simply, on a sheet of aluminium foil on the baking tray.
If you actually make the figures on the aluminium foil this means that you do not have to lift them from it. This is particularly convenient when you are handling delicate figures.
Make sure that the aluminium foil is dull side up if you are using it in an electric oven, as the shiny side could interfere with the thermostat in the oven.

Temperature
For the best results the temperature inside the oven should be raised gradually during the baking process.
If the oven is too hot, this can lead to crumbling or burning.
If the dough has been left to dry for some time beforehand it is generally alright to start with an oven temperature of 150°C. If you wish to dry the figure in the oven, it is usually better to begin with a lower temperature of about 100°C. for about 30 minutes, leaving the door of the oven slightly ajar so that the damp air can escape.
When the surface of the dough starts to feel firm it is time to increase the temperature in the oven gradually up to about 250°C. Thin, flat figures will reach this stage earlier than solid, compact figures. For this reason it is important to keep a careful eye on the dough at the beginning. To check on the hardness of the figures, it will certainly need no more than keeping the door open.
There is a possibility that during the first quarter of an hour that the dough is baking, air bubbles will appear on the surface of the figure. As the dough is still soft at this stage you can carefully prick these blisters with a needle and smooth them with your finger.
It is not possible to give a temperature which will be suitable for all figures. The temperature always depends on the thickness and the shape of the individual figures. Obviously a small, flat figure cannot tolerate temperatures as high as a large, compact figure. Moreover, the temperature also depends on the shade of brown you wish to obtain.

Baking time
The baking time also depends on the type of dough figures concerned and the shade of brown you want the figures to be.
Small figures, such as bread dolls or lockets etc. generally only need baking for 30 or 40 minutes. Slightly larger figures, such as wall decorations, will take approximately 60-90 minutes to bake, while large, compact pieces, such as upright figures and garlands, will take up to 2 or 3 hours.
In general, coloured dough or dough made from rye flour will take longer to bake than dough made from plain white flour. It is possible to shorten the baking time by moving the figures from the baking tray directly onto the metal grid in the oven, once they are hard

enough. In this way the bottom also becomes very hot. As stated above, the shade of brown required is also related to the baking time. If you want to achieve a good deep brown colour, the figure usually has to stay in the oven for a longer time. If you wish to paint the entire figure after baking it, it only needs to be light brown and can be taken out of the oven sooner.

The most important thing to remember is that after baking the figures they should be absolutely dry and rock-hard.

Painting the figures

Obviously you do not have to paint your figures after baking them. The beautiful shades of brown which can be obtained simply by baking can be at least as attractive as the colours obtained by painting the figures.

Nevertheless, many people decide to decorate their figures with vivid colours, and there are various ways of doing this.

Always make sure that the figures are quite hard and completely cool before using either paint or varnish.

Watercolours
First, there is the possibility of using watercolours to do the painting. Many people prefer watercolours because this type of paint preserves the characteristic qualities of the dough once it has been baked: the crystalline, shiny effect of the surface of the dough.

However, a disadvantage of using watercolours is that the paint can be absorbed by the dough, producing very pale colours. In addition, there is a possibility that the various adjacent layers of paint could merge together producing unsightly grey areas.

This can be largely prevented by covering the bread sculpture first with a layer of white paint. Ordinary white watercolours can be used for this, counteracting the absorbent quality of the dough so that the next layer of paint takes better.

Acrylic paint
The problems mentioned above of colours merging together or the paint being absorbed, obviously do not arise with acrylic paints, which work rather like varnish.

Acrylic paints can be used to produce much more vivid colours than watercolours. Moreover, acrylic paints are easier to use, the paint does not disappear into the dough, and if you make a mistake, it is much easier to correct it. Particularly when you have not yet mastered the art of painting your figures, it is generally better and more precise to work with acrylic paints.

Before you start using the paint it is always advisable to remember that light colours are more easy to change to dark colours, though you could have problems the other way round. Therefore it is best to start with light colours. In addition, mixing colours requires a technique that is not mastered just like that.

It is worth spending an hour mixing the paints from different tubes until you obtain the colour you require.

You can produce an attractive effect by mixing a number of different shades from one basic colour such as pink, pale red, scarlet or dark red.

You can create shadows in the figures by using slightly thicker layers of paint in the folds.

If the paint has been applied too thickly or incorrectly in certain places, it could help to cover these parts with a layer of white paint before painting over them a second time. If you wish to paint the whole figure again, it is best to varnish it first and then paint over this with white watercolour paint.

A coloured effect without using paint
As stated above, it is certainly not necessary to use paint to obtain some beautiful colours. If you are content to use the many shades of brown obtained by means of the various baking techniques, it is possible to achieve some splendid results.

Even when you let nature have her own way, some beautiful shades are guaranteed after baking because the raised and lower parts of the figure will be heated to a different degree and therefore also turn a different colour.

If you want to produce a deep brown colour in certain places, it is a good idea to brush some milk over these areas before baking the figure. An even deeper shade of brown can be obtained by brushing a little oil over the required areas. Obviously you can also produce darker and lighter colours by turning the oven higher or lower. However, when you turn the oven temperature up, you should always watch out for burning. It is particularly important to keep a careful check when using the 'grill' position.

If you want certain parts of the figure to remain a very light brown colour, these can be covered in advance, or while the figure is baking, with pieces of aluminium foil. Afterwards, carefully remove the pieces of foil, preferably only when the figure has thoroughly cooled.

If you do not paint your figure, you will still have to make sure that you protect it against damp. The large amount of salt in the dough means that when the figure is exposed to the air, it will attract moisture, and this results in it becoming soft and rather shapeless.

Apply a layer of varnish to the surface and you will save yourself a lot of trouble later on.

Finishing off the figures

Obviously you will wish to enjoy your handwork made of dough for a long time to come. It is therefore important to know what to do to protect the figures. Take particular care with regard to the following points:

– The fact that the salt in the dough *strongly attracts* moisture was mentioned above. To prevent your figures going soft and shapeless as a result of damp, it is best to apply a coat of varnish first.
Obviously you must also make sure that you do not display the figures in a damp spot or hang them on a damp wall.

If you are not sure whether the walls are damp, make doubly sure of protecting any wall decorations by sticking a layer of felt or aluminium foil on the back.
If the damage has already been done and your bread sculpture is affected by damp, it is possible to bake it again at a low temperature after carrying out the necessary repairs.

– Figures painted with poster paints are usually sufficiently protected against damp, but nevertheless need a coat of varnish to protect the colours from fading. Obviously this also applies for figures painted with watercolours.
Another easy way of preventing the colours from fading is with a layer of wax. You can submerge the entire figure in a basin of hot wax so that the surface of the figure acquires a beautiful pearly sheen.

– If, when you handle the figure with great care, it still happens that part of it crumbles away or that the figure actually breaks for some reason, there's no need to panic, for in many cases it is possible to repair the damage. Stick the pieces together with a little water or even with some ordinary glue; then bake the figure again at a low temperature.

A decorated heart

There is probably no shape as evocative and with such appeal to the imagination as the heart shape. This is as it should be, for the heart is not only the most important and even essential organ for both humans and animals, it is also generally recognized as being the seat of the most intense human emotions: love, friendship, sympathy, courage – not to mention fear. Thus it is not without reason that the heart is sometimes identified with man's whole personality.

The heart has been used since time immemorial to express elevated and abstract feelings. Essentially the heart is a symbol for human feelings, and is seen as the counter balance to the intelligence, which is seated in the head or the brain.

Therefore it is not surprising that there are phrases and proverbs based on the heart in every language.

To mention just a few: 'to wear your heart on your sleeve' (not hiding your emotions); 'not having your heart in it' (not really wanting to do something); 'with your heart in your mouth' (fear). Many novelists have used imagery based on the heart, usually to describe certain feelings or atmospheres; his heart stopped, she had a broken heart, or her heart skipped a beat. The advertising industry also often makes use of the word or the shape of a heart to make a product more attractive.

The heart made from dough that is described in this chapter has a very basic shape. If you prefer a simple, unadorned design you might leave the design as it is, with at most a slight emphasis here and there. For example, you might use an arrow through the heart (Cupid's arrow) or engrave a name or a saying in the dough in flowery lettering. As mentioned above, there are many sayings and proverbs based on the heart, but obviously you could also choose a suitable and original saying of your own.

Those people who like decoration and more complicated projects will find that they can use this basic shape in all sorts of ways. The heart can be decorated with all sorts of objects, such as dried flowers, beads, ribbons or buttons. It could also serve as a basis for a small tableau, surrounded, for example, by small figures or rosettes of dough. Finally it is also possible to engrave a drawing on the heart, which can later be given some relief by raising some parts of the design with extra dough.

In this first chapter the preparation of the dough is once more clearly described with a series of photographs. Further details regarding the preparation of the dough can be found in the introductory chapters.

The use of the rolling pin to roll out thin or thick slabs of dough is also explained. Obviously many different shapes can be cut out from the dough.

By far the easiest way is to use aluminium pastry cutters which are available in all sorts of different shapes and sizes. If you wish to cut out a rather unusual shape, it is a good idea to draw the design on paper first. If you do use pastry cutters the edges of the figure will probably be ragged. The best thing to do is to rub over the edges with a wet finger until they are quite smooth.

1
Lay out all the tools and ingredients.

2
Use the same cup and measuring jug for all the ingredients. Start with the flour.

3
To make this figure, put three cups of flour in the mixing bowl.

4
Add one cup of salt to the flour and mix the two dry ingredients.

5
Now add one cup of water to the mixture.

6
Finally, add a splash of glycerine to the mixture.

7
Knead the mixture of flour, salt, water and glycerine thoroughly.

8
Continue kneading the dough until it forms a firm ball with no air bubbles.

9

Press the ball of dough flat on a wooden board.

10

Roll out the dough to the required size with a rolling pin.

11

Cut out a heart shape from the sheet of paper and lie this on the dough. Press down gently.

12

Cut out the heart shape with a sharp knife. Do not press too hard with the hand which is keeping the paper heart in its place.

13

Remove the dough which has been cut away and carefully remove the paper heart shape from the dough.

14

With a flat knife carefully lift the heart and transfer to a baking try covered in aluminium foil (dull side up).

15

The rough edges of the heart can be smoothed out with a wet finger. Roll an oval ball of dough in the palm of your hand. This ball is stuck just below the centre of the heart with a few drops of water.

16

Roll out two long coils of dough of the same thickness on the board.

17

Plait the two rolls together to form a cord.

18

Place the dough cord around the oval ball so that the ends of the cord do not quite touch. The dough under the cord is made slightly wet in advance.

19

The space between the two ends of the cord is filled with berries or apples – small balls of dough.

20

To make the balls of dough look like real berries or apples, prick on one side with a skewer. This is where the stalk has been twisted off.

21

Make the leaves for the flowers from a flat piece of dough. With a small knife draw in the veins of the leaf to make it look real.

22

Carefully press a stalk for the leaf by pressing together the dough between the thumb and forefinger. (Note the way the veins of the leaf are pointing.) The leaves are attached to the heart with water in the same way as the berries.

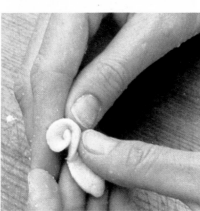

23

Small rosettes are made from a flat, rectangular piece of dough rolled up between the thumb and forefinger. Press down on one end of the rolled up piece of dough so that the other end opens wider.

24

Arrange the rosettes to your liking and stick down with water.

25

Stick down as many berries, leaves, rosettes and other decorations as you think are necessary. The surface of this heart is completely covered with decorations.

26

Meanwhile prick an opening in the heart with a cocktail stick so that the heart can be hung up on a ribbon or length of cord.

27

The modelling is now complete and the heart can be slid into the oven on the baking tray. Bake slowly (approximately 3 hours at regulo mark 2-3, 150°C.-180°C.) until the heart is a golden brown colour.

28

When it has cooled down the heart can be painted with watercolours or acrylic paints. When it is complete, apply a coat of transparant varnish to protect the dough against damp. This is not necessary if acrylic paints have been used.

A very individual fish

Since time immemorial animals have been assigned different symbolic meanings in different parts of the world.

For example, the lion is known for its courage, the fox for its cunning, the owl for its wisdom and the snake for its baseness. Fish also acquired a particular symbolic significance very early on because fish have always been one of the most important sources of food.

The most well-known significance of fish is in astrology. Pisces is one of the twelve signs of the zodiac, and various characteristics, such as sensitivity, indecisiveness, a propensity to self-sacrifice and a tendency to escape are just some of the attributes of this sign.

The fish crops up as an important figure in biblical stories, as well as in numerous fairytales, for example, in the story of the prophet Jonah who spent three days and nights inside a whale. Probably the universally popular tale of the puppet Pinocchio and his father was based on the biblical legend. Pinocchio too was caught in the stomach of a whale, though he eventually managed to escape on the back of another helpful fish.

Another example is the flounder, which plays a very important role in the fairytale of the same name by the brothers Grimm.

Fish can still be considered today as one of the most important sources of food for mankind, but in addition, fish also provide one of the most popular leisure activities. The annual opening of the fishing season always sees large numbers of keen anglers getting out their rods. Apart from this there are many beautiful aquarium fish which are the pride and joy of many a proud aquarium owner.

It is not for nothing that we have chosen to make a fish out of dough in this chapter, for the fish is a beautiful creature. It has a characteristic shape with its gills, fins and scales, which come in all shapes and sizes and can be modelled very easily in dough.

1

Sprinkle some flour onto a wooden board and roll out the dough. Use a glass to cut out a circle from the dough.

2

Cut out the circle with a sharp knife.

3

Carefully remove the excess dough which has been cut away.

4

Smooth the edge of the circle with a wet finger.

5

Draw the head of the fish, though without cutting too deeply, with the blunt edge of a knife.

6

Cut a small triangle out of the circle. This forms the mouth.

7

Cut the tail, the dorsal fin and the pectoral fin from flat pieces of dough in a semi-circle.

8

Stick the tail and the fins to the body of the fish with water.

9

With a modelling tool draw in the patterns for the tail and fins.

10

Prick small holes in the body of the fish with a cocktail stick to prevent air bubbles forming when the fish is baked.

11

Make small balls of dough and press flat to form the scales.

12

Arrange the scales by sliding slightly underneath the next ones (like roof tiles) and stick to the body with water.

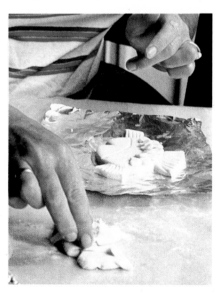

13

Make an eye from a small ball of dough and moisten the place where it is stuck on the head. Draw in the pattern round the open mouth with a stick.

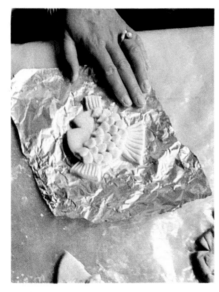

14

Start with the little boy. For the head roll a nice round ball of dough. Make two indentations in this ball with the rounded end of a modelling tool and then prick two holes in these with a cocktail stick. These are the eyes.

15

Make the nose and mouth from very small balls of dough and with a cocktail stick position these on the face after wetting it slightly.

16

Make a cylindrical body.

17

Carefully press the body against the head with a stick. Make sure you wet the place where they join first.

18

Model the breeches and attach to the body with water.

19
Stick the whole body of the boy on the back of the fish behind the pectoral fin, with a few drops of water.

20
Fashion a hook from some wire and carefully prick this through the top of the boy's head. The hook should go halfway into the body of the boy.

21
Make some hair using a garlic press and stick it onto the head with water.

22
Fashion two sleeves (arms) and attach them to the body with water.

23
Make two mittens and notch in the fingers with a cocktail stick. Then attach to the sleeves with water. Fashion a foot and attach to the breeches with water.

24
This individual fish is now complete and ready to bake in the oven.

Like two peas in a pod

Like the fish (Pisces) in the previous chapter, twins (Gemini) is another sign of the zodiac. In general the characteristics of this sign are considered to include lively, spirited, social and subtle traits.

Twins have always engendered enormous fascination. In fact they are both a mythological phenomenon, as well as one that occurs in reality.

Twins are born to humans and mammals; they develop together during pregnancy and are born one shortly after the other. Among human beings each of the children is known as a twin.

There are actually two different types of twins: identical (monozygotic) twins and twins which are not identical. (bizygotic). When they are not identical the twins are as likely to resemble one another as two brothers, two sisters or a brother and a sister. When the twins are a boy and a girl they can be desribed as a 'twin couple'.

However, identical twins develop from a single cell; these twins are always the same sex and are generally as alike as two peas in a pod. In fact, this resemblance is not confined to external characteristics but often also extends to various important character traits. Usually identical twins are great fun to watch, especially when the children are small and their mother dresses them identically. This similarity between two children or two adults has provided endless material for comical situations and combinations both in films and literature, and in real life.

1

Sprinkle the wooden board with flour and roll out a cylindrical piece of dough, tapering to a point at one end. Do this by pressing down on this end while you are rolling.

2

Cut away the broad end with a knife.

3

Repeat this procedure with another piece of dough of the same shape. These form the bodies of the twins.

4

Roll two perfectly round balls of dough for the heads.

5

Join one of the balls to the body with some water.

6

Then do the same with the other ball. Place the figures at an angle towards each other but so that the heads do not touch.

7
Fashion two hooks from a piece of wire and prick through the tops of the heads into the bodies. Make sure that the hooks are the same length as the figures.

8
With the fingers make two indentations for the eye sockets halfway up the head.

9
Prick holes in the eye sockets with the blunt end of a cocktail stick. These are the eyes.

10
Make the nose and mouth from balls of dough and with a cocktail stick, stick these onto the head, after wetting the right places. Prick two holes in each nose.

11
Roll out a piece of dough into a flat layer.

12
Cut a wide strip from this layer. This will be the skirt.

13
Cut the strip at an angle at both ends. Then cut the same shape for the other skirt.

14
Arrange the skirts in pleats after wetting the bodies, so that they only cover half of the bodies.

15
Place the skirts so that they are touching along the side and stick together with water.

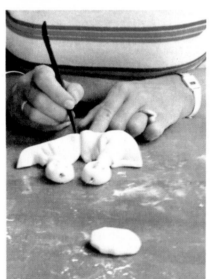

16
Cut the bodices of the dresses from a thin piece of dough.

17
Fit the bodices onto the figure. Smooth out the edges of the small triangles with a wet finger.

18
Attach the bodices round the figures with some water.

19

When the bodice and skirt of the dress are joined together, make some small holes in the waist (just above the pleated edge) with a modelling tool.

20

Roll four cylinders for the arms.

21

Attach the arms to the bodies with water. Use the modelling tool to prevent the arms from being stiffly held against the bodies.

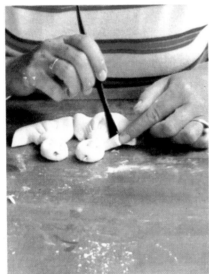

22

Fashion some mittens from the dough and carve in the fingers with a cocktail stick. Then attach the mittens to the arms with a wet finger and a modelling tool.

23

Put a small lump of dough in the garlic press and press slowly.

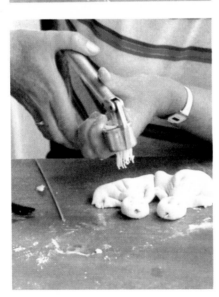

24

Press the garlic press completely shut so that long strands of dough are pressed out. These can be used for the hair.

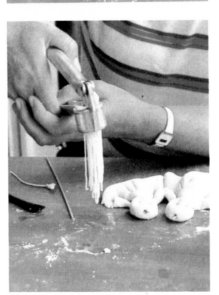

25

With a modelling tool carefully stick the hairs to the head after wetting them.

26

Cut two triangles for the hats from a thin piece of dough.

27

One of the hats is stuck onto the head with some water.

28

The same procedure is followed for the other hat. Then press the two hats carefully together. Make them wet first.

29

Use a modelling tool to take out the two hooks by pulling them through the hats.

30

Roll out a piece of dough.

31
Fashion a foot from it.

32
Stick the foot down under the skirt with a few drops of water. Do the same for the other three feet.

33
The twins are now ready to be baked in the oven.

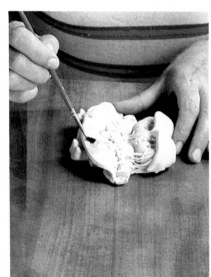

34
When they have been baked you can paint the figures according to taste with watercolours or acrylic paints.

35
When the figures have been painted, cover with a protective coat of varnish and attach a small chain to the hooks.

A miniature cradle

The cradle that is copied in this chapter is a very old-fashioned model. It is the so-called hanging cradle, the oldest type of cradle known in the Netherlands, which was in common use between 1300 and 1600.

The cradle was not always the place where newborn babies were laid down to sleep. Before 1300 it had been common practice for centuries for babies to sleep in their parents' bed at night. In the daytime a baby would usually be swaddled (in swaddling clothes) and laid in a basket or a wooden box. However, it could be quite dangerous for a baby to sleep in bed with its parents; it occasionally happened that the parents would turn in their sleep on top of their child. Eventually it was actually forbidden by law for a young baby to sleep in bed with its parents.

A type of 'crib chest' or even a 'baby drawer' beneath the parents' bed was one step closer to the cradle.

The hanging cradle was followed by a new model – the rocking cradle; a cradle which could be rocked with either the hand or the foot. A 'cradle string' was soon introduced for convenience. This was a length of string attached at one end to the edge of the cradle and at the other, around the nurse's wrist. In this way the cradle rocked in time with the movements of her arm as she sat knitting or crocheting, humming lullabyes or nursery rhymes dreamily at the same time.

The rocking cradle was widely used up to the middle of the last century despite various warnings from medical quarters that the rocking action was harmful for a newborn baby.

Nowadays the most common type of crib is a cradle that stands on four legs, though sometimes the actual bassinet is suspended so that it can still rock.

This model also dates back a long way and has gradually replaced other models which were used in the past.

The small cradle made of dough in our example obviously looks very attractive when it is hung in the hood of a large cradle, and it makes an original present for the birth of a baby. In this way the old-fashioned hanging cradle still finds its place in the nursery in a miniature form. If there is no room in the actual cradle, it also looks very attractive as a wall decoration or makes a suitable toy in the playpen.

1
Sprinkle flour on the wooden board and roll out a ball of dough with the rolling pin.

2
Cut the bassinet of the cradle from this piece of dough. It has two sloping sides.

3
Roll out another piece of dough.

4
Cut the top of the cradle from this second piece of dough. This shape is slightly longer than the bottom of the cradle. Stick the top of the cradle to the bassinet with a few drops of water.

5
Fashion a hook from a piece of wire and push into the dough at the top of the cradle.

6
Cut a coverlet from a piece of dough; this is a long, thin, rectangular piece of dough. Stick onto the basinet with a few drops of water.

7 Roll out a piece of dough very thinly.

8 Cut straight along the top and bottom of this piece of dough.

9 Cut off the other two sides at an angle. This forms the basis of the curtain.

10 Cut the shape into two pieces.

11 Pleat the curtains and attach to the top of the cradle, first wetting the point at which the curtain is joined.

12 Put some extra folds in the top of the curtains with a modelling tool.

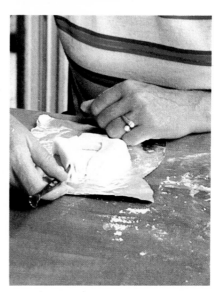

13

Roll a perfectly round piece of dough.

14

About halfway up, press an eye socket in the ball of dough with the rounded end of the modelling tool.

15

Press the second eye socket at the same level.

16

Make a nose from a very small piece of dough. Wet the spot where it is to be attached and stick down on the head. Prick two holes in the nose with a cocktail stick.

17

Put a small ball of dough on the face to form the mouth with a cocktail stick. Then press lightly so that the lips pout slightly.

18

Prick holes in the eye sockets to form the eyes.

19
Make strands of head with a garlic press; wet the head and stick the hair onto the head.

20
Stick the hair down with water between the curtains.

21
Drape the curtains around the head.

22
Fashion two little mittens from a small piece of dough and stick these down on the sheet with wet fingers.

23
Make lines in the mittens with a modelling tool to form the fingers.

24
Emphasize the pleats at the bottom of the curtains with the modelling tool.

25
Pleat the inner edges of the curtains with the fingers and a modelling tool.

26
Make a coil of dough for the rockers of the cradle.

27
Cut to size (about 1½ times the width of the bottom of the cradle) and flatten the coil slightly.

28
Bend the rocker slightly and attach to the bottom of the cradle with some water.

29
Make horizontal lines in the bassinet with a modelling tool.

30
Roll out a piece of dough very thinly.

31

Cut a narrow strip from this piece of dough.

32

Fashion this strip of dough into a ribbon.

33

Attach the strip to the top of the cradle with water.

34

The cradle is now finished.

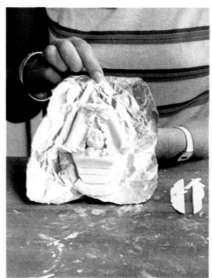

35

Switch on the oven and slide the cradle inside. Bake slowly.

36

When the cradle is baked paint in the desired colours in watercolours or acrylic paints. Then cover with a protective coat of varnish.

Babe in nappy

When you see this baby in its nappy made from dough, it reminds you immediately of the traditional stork.

This is the age-old fable about the stork delivering a baby to the expecting mother, wrapped beautifully in a nappy which the stork carries in its beak.

Nowadays not many children are given this type of misleading sex information, but in the past every child was invariably told this tale every time a brother or sister was born into the family and the inevitable question arose: 'Munny, where did that baby come from?' Obviously there were also other common explanations to clarify the sudden appearance of the newcomer, such as the gooseberry bush or the rhubarb patch, where babies could sometimes be found.

The stork only actually appeared in stories as the bringer of babes in the 17th and 18th centuries.

Before this the bird was generally considered to be a bringer of good luck, and wherever a stork nested, the house would be protected from lightning and fire and the midwives were safe from danger.

When the stork became a symbol of procreation and the bringer of babies, the story ran that it had plucked the baby from a special baby tree, or that it had enchanted a frog it had caught and turned it into a baby. The first version is undoubtedly related to the myth of the tree of life, to which we return later on in the book. The latter version is possibly related to the almost scientific 'frog test' used earlier this century as a pregnancy test. Whatever the truth of the matter, the stork brought the baby to the expectant mother and obviously this required a nappy which the stork held in its beak.

For a long time it seemed that storks might disappear from the Netherlands altogether, but a group of nature lovers acted successfully to prevent this, and recently more storks

have been seen there than ever before. In many places tall posts were planted with wagon wheels on top to attract storks and encourage them to nest.

Like the cradle made from dough in the last chapter, this baby in its nappy makes an appropriate gift at the birth of a baby. At the same time, the baby is an ode to the many fairytales told about the stork, the wonderful bringer of good fortune, who is making a more regular appearance nowadays.

1
Take a piece of dough.

2
Sprinkle some flour on a wooden board.

3
Roll out the dough thinly.

4
Cut the dough with a sharp knife.

5
Cut a diamond shape from the dough with a knife. This forms the nappy.

6
Remove the excess dough which has been cut away.

7
Roll a cylinder tapering to a point at one end (the body).

8
Place the cylinder in the middle of the nappy.

9
Fold one of the points of the nappy over the body.

10
Press down the two points of the nappy after wetting them. The bottom of the nappy should be kept open.

11
Make some fine pleats in the point of the nappy with a cocktail stick.

12
Make a few pleats in the bottom of the nappy with a modelling tool.

13
Roll out a perfectly round ball of dough.

14
Press the eye sockets in the ball with the fingers.

15
Prick holes in the eye sockets with a cocktail stick for the eyes.

16
Stick onto the head a small ball of dough with a cocktail stick for the nose after wetting this point on the ball. Prick two nostrils in the nose.

17
Stick on another small ball of dough with the cocktail stick to form the mouth. Make sure that you wet the right place first and press a hole in the mouth.

18
Make some hair with the garlic press and press onto the head after wetting it.

19
Press the nappy open on both sides with a modelling tool.

20
Stick the head down in the nappy with water.

21
Roll two short cylinders of dough and fashion them into legs and feet.

22
Put the legs into the nappy and stick down with water.

23
Press a wire hook into the dough through the top of the nappy. Cover the hook with a small triangle of dough pressed into the top of the nappy and stuck down with water.

24
Press the join between the triangle and the nappy shut with a cocktail stick.

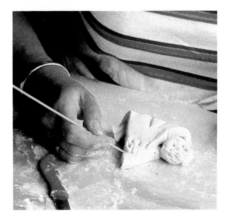

25
Press a narrow strip of dough on the bottom of the triangle with a damp finger.

26
The baby is now finished and is placed on a sheet of aluminium foil.

27
Slide into the oven on a baking tray and bake slowly.

28
The baby in its nappy after baking, ready to be painted and varnished according to taste.

The Dutch 'gaper' a form of free sculpture

The Dutch 'gaper' was originally the symbol of one of the guilds, though it was not adopted as such until the end of the seventeenth century, long after the first guilds had been founded in the Netherlands.

Initially a guild was an association of tradesmen, such as bakers or carpenters, who used a particular symbol to advertise their profession. These guild signs originated at a time when most people could not read, and a symbol was therefore the easiest way to identify a particular shop or workshop.

The oldest known gaper dates from 1693, and was used by an apothecary in the town of Middelburg. It must have been round about this time that apothecaries increasingly began to make use of this specific sign on a board, and this trend was later adopted by many chemists. Actually the gaper was not the only symbol used by apothecaries, for in many places in the Netherlands the mortar and pestle was the symbol used to denote this profession.

It is not really very clear why so many apothecaries chose the characteristic gaper figure. It is assumed that the figure served to attract the attention of passers by. Some of the heads were certainly very bizarre. For example, there was a jester's head, a head with a helmet, or one with a crown or garland.

You could even come across a gaper wearing a tall top hat, eerily similar to an undertaker's hat.

The most common and probably the best known gaper is the black head of a Moor or 'Musulman', always bedecked in a brightly coloured turban or another type of extravagant headdress.

Although the gaper heads throughout the Netherlands vary enormously, they are always the head of a man with his mouth wide open, as though this indicates that the pills manufactured in that shop and the potions concocted there, were of the best quality and absolutely essential for good health. When you can actually see the tongue of the gaper sticking out, you might imagine that the physician has made his diagnosis and has referred the patient to this particular apothecary for a remedy for the complaint.

The characteristic gapers which could once be admired in any village or town in the Netherlands are gradually disappearing from the shop fronts. About a hundred now remain throughout the country. The tax – known as 'precario tax' – which was levied at the beginning of the century on signs or other symbols hanging outside the shop fronts over the public highway, led many apothecaries and chemists to remove their beautiful gaper heads or to find a place for them indoors.

Another reason for bringing the heads inside was the growing possibility that these antiques might be stolen – not to mention the danger of damage by vandals.

Moreover, some shopkeepers might have been afraid that the beautifully carved wooden heads would be damaged by the effect of wind and rain. Finally, it is impossible to ignore the fact that advertisements in electric light or neon are much more striking nowadays and possibly these have replaced the authentic gaper.

When you are making a gaper as a bread sculpture, this is an art form in which your imagination can run riot. As mentioned above, the gaper appears in many guises and there is no reason why you should restrict yourself to the familiar Moor's head. You are free to make any sort of head, wearing any sort of headdress, as long as the mouth is wide open. You should not forget to make the tongue stick out, for this feature really serves to remind you of the apothecary and the miracles his pills would hopefully bring about.

These beautiful gapers served as models for the examples described
in the chapter.

For this head you will need 3½ cups of flour, 1 cup of salt and a small amount of water. Add a little bit of glycerine.

1
You need a firm dough for the gaper. Use a greater proportion of flour when preparing the dough than you did for the dough used in the previous chapters.

2
Put the dough in a rounded oval shape on a baking tray. The top should be more rounded than the bottom which tapers to a slightly pointed end.

3
Press the eye sockets in the dough with the fingers.

4
Fashion a nose and moustache according to your own taste. Press down onto the face keeping the fingers wet.

5
Make the nostrils with the pointed end of a paintbrush.

6
Fashion the upper lip and stick down with wet fingers.

7
Carefully smooth the parts of the face you have added with wet fingers.

8
Make the opening for the mouth by pressing two fingers into the dough.

9
Make the chin and smooth out the joins with wet fingers.

10
Get rid of uneven areas with small pieces of dough.

11
Form the lower lip from a thin strip of dough, keeping the fingers wet.

12
Stick down a strip of dough inside the mouth with wet fingers and mark in the teeth with a sharp knife.

13
Small almond shaped pieces of dough are stuck down in the sockets to form the eyes. Keep the fingers wet.

14
Stick down thin slivers of dough above and below the eyes with wet fingers. These form the eyelashes.

15
Roll out a thick layer of dough for the turban and fold this roll around the head.

16
Press pleats into the turban with a cocktail stick.

17
Press the turban against the head with wet fingers.

18
Press the pleats in the turban again with the cocktail stick.

19
Smooth out the join between the head and the turban with the rounded end of a paintbrush.

20
Decorate the turban with small balls of dough. Keep the fingers wet.

21
Roll out a thick cylinder of dough for the beard.

22
Now stick down the cylinder of dough on the chin with wet fingers in such a way that the ends of the cylinder of dough touch the turban.

23
Suggest the structure of a rough beard in the cylinder of dough, using a cocktail stick.

24

You can create a rough surface by passing the cocktail stick flat over the entire beard.

25

For the tongue, make a slice of dough and stick down in the mouth with the fingers.

26

Finally put the finishing touches to the head according to taste. Keep the fingers wet.

27

When the figure has been baked, accentuate the eyes with watercolours or acrylic paints.

28

Then paint the gaper according to taste. Finish with a protective coat of varnish.

Creating different surfaces

To make attractive patterns in dough you can use all sorts of different objects. It is easy to draw on a smooth piece of dough used as the basis for a whole scene, with a pointed object such as a cocktail stick, a nail or a needle.

Any object you consider suitable can be used for decorating dough figures with all sorts of decorative patterns: a piece of lace, a key, leaves, a screw, a spool, a shell and even special stamps made for the purpose.

1 Lie the leaf of a tree or a plant on a piece of dough. Do not use a dried out leaf.

2 Transfer the pattern of the leaf onto the dough by rolling over it with a bottle.

3
Roll the dough so that it is completely flat.

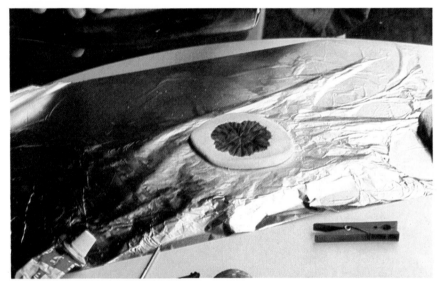

4
The leaf on the dough after it has been rolled with the bottle.

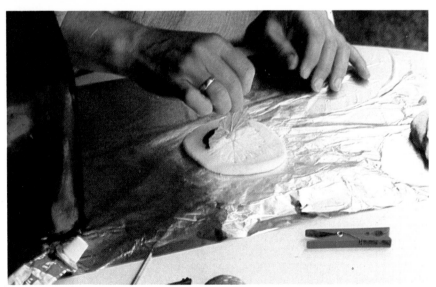

5
Carefully remove the leaf from the dough.

6 Making a pattern by pressing down the bottom part of a key.

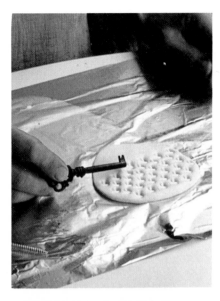

7 Carefully press the screw into the dough lengthways.

8 The head of a screw or a nail can create an attractive pattern of circles. It is also possible to combine different sizes.

9 This shell can be used to make a crinkly pattern by pressing down the edge into the dough.

10 This pattern is made with the end of a steel skewer.

11 The side of a sewing machine spool can also be used to make an attractive pattern.

12
Place a strip of lace on a large piece of dough.

13
Roll a bottle over the lace to transfer the pattern of the lace onto the dough.

14
The pattern on the dough when the lace has been carefully removed.

15 Make a semi-circular ball of dough.

16 Press eye sockets into the dough with the thumbs.

17 The same action seen from the right.

18 Press eyes into the sockets with the end of a steel skewer.

19 Press the eyebrows in the dough with the end of a key.

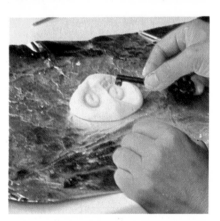

20 Make a feathery pattern on the mask using the thread of a screw.

21 Press the nose with a clothespeg.

22 The mask is ready to be baked.

A swaddling child

In the days when houses were not quite as draught-free as nowadays, and it was important to protect newborn children from the cold, swaddling clothes were an important part of child care. The painting De Dordtse Vierling, by an unknown artist in the 17th century, clearly shows a number of typically swaddled children.

It depicts four newborn babies, three of whom are firmly swaddled in very richly decorated swaddling clothes so that only their faces are visible. The fourth child in the painting is lying on a cushion and wearing a white shroud; it died at birth.

The rich embroidery on the swaddling clothes suggests that not only poor families living in poorly insulated, barely heated homes used swaddling clothes, but that the babies of prosperous families were also swaddled. It was generally considered in those days that a baby's skin was for too delicate to be exposed to the air.

In the past babies were looked after most of the time by a nurse, the equivalent of the modern midwife.

She would look after both mother and child and would often come to live in the home of the expecting mother some time before the birth, to help with the housework and get to know the other children in the family.

As soon as the baby was born it was immediately wrapped up in swaddling clothes by the nurse. The arms would be pressed tight against the body so that heat loss was kept to a minimum, and the baby was tightly swaddled.

The swaddling clothes were changed only once a day, so that they served as a nappy and as the baby's clothes at the same time.

The mother was usually weak and needed to sleep without being woken up by a crying baby, so the nurse would often take the swaddled baby home with her in the evening and it would sleep in her bed, as there was rarely a nursery in those days. The following day the nurse would bring the baby back home to mother.

As described in the chapter on cradles, the nurse would put the baby, swaddling clothes and all, in a hanging or rocking cradle during the day, or sometimes in a simple wicker basket or wooden box. The nurse would constantly sing lullabyes or nursery rhymes while she worked – cleaning the house, mending clothes, peeling potatoes or cooking the meal, for in those days the nurse did everything in the home. Obviously some nurses were not of such a musical disposition, but most women who took up this work put their whole heart into it. The nurses knew many traditional lullabyes, which were meant to soothe a crying baby or make it laugh.

There were some simple songs, but also a number of fairly complicated rhymes; dancing or counting rhymes.

The soporific lullabyes which the nurse would sing as she rocked the cradle would send mother and baby off into a deep sleep. Most of these rhymes no longer exist or have changed so much in the course of time that the original words have become obscured.

To return to the habit of swaddling babies, the subject of this chapter – this was common practice in many countries such as Spain, for example. There they used strips of material rather than swaddling clothes.

The baby's arms, legs and body were wrapped up firmly in the bandage because it was feared that a young child's limbs could easily break if they simply hung 'loose'.

Nowadays the habit of swaddling babies only survives in Eastern countries. In these countries the standard of living, medical aid and hygiene are still in a very early stage of development and the swaddling clothes still serve a useful purpose. For most children there is no warm, safe cradle, let alone a comfortably heated home.

In our own country only the shape of the cradle and of the baby's pram is reminiscent of the original swaddling clothes. They 'cradle' the child within the oval shape and provide a cover for the child's head, just as in the old days. Fortunately these modern 'swaddling clothes' allow the child a lot more freedom of movement.

1

A homogeneous ball of dough with no air remaining inside it is placed on the work surface. (A wooden board covered with aluminium foil.)

2

Press the ball flat and fashion into the body of a baby.

3

Roll out a ball of dough and stick it to the rest of the body with some water. This is the baby's head.

4

For the hair press a piece of dough through the garlic press. Then arrange the hair round the head and stick down with water.

5

Cover a roll of dough with a sheet of transparent cling film. This stops the dough from sticking to the rolling pin.

6

Roll out the dough thinly.

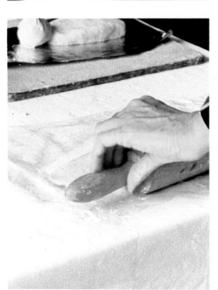

7

Remove the cling film and cut the cape for the head from the piece of dough.

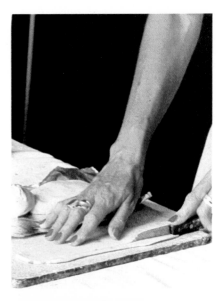

8

Put the cape round the head, sticking it down with some water.

9

Press the cape against the body with wet fingers.

10

Cut the eyes by making slits in the face with a sharp knife.

11

Shape the mouth from a small ball of dough. Stick down with wet fingers and make an incision for the lips with a sharp knife.

12

Example of a pattern made with a number of different buttons.

13
Decorate the body with a pattern, for example, using buttons. Also see the chapter on how to make different patterns.

14
Draw or press a decorative pattern on the body with a skewer.

15
Use the skewer to make a pattern of your own choice around the edge of the cape.

16
Using a modelling tool, press short lines round the edge of the cape.

17
Finish off the baby with swaddling clothes using modelling tools and your own imagination.

A garland of flowers

Garlands have been used as a symbol of victory and triumph in every culture since time immemorial. More than two thousand years ago garlands were generally used to crown people as a sign of distinction and honour when they performed a particularly laudable deed, and this custom continues to the present day.

Nowadays top sportsmen and women are still garlanded with beautiful wreaths as a sign of their success.

Even animals on the sporting world such as greyhounds, or horses in steeplechasing and other sorts of horseracing are often given garlands of flowers when they win.

The significance of the garland as a sign of victory is related to the holy meaning that has always been attributed to the circle. In many religions the circle returns as the symbol of the span of life; from birth to death, and – in some cases – from death to rebirth.

The changing seasons and the cycles in nature also reveal this circularity which is related to all life on earth.

Quite probably the wheel of adventure and the wheel of fortune at the funfair can also be viewed in the light of life which alternately brings good fortune and misfortune. Though garlands are usually used in cases of good luck and success, the symbol can also be regarded in the wider context of the meaning of the circle; as a symbol of life and all that occurs in it. Surely the best way to honour a person who has been victorious is with this symbol of life.

In most cases the garlands were made of plants, twigs, flowers and leaves plaited together. The Greeks and Romans used laurel twigs to plait their laurel wreaths.

These were usually small wreaths worn as a crown by victorious gladiators or soldiers or other successful people such as poets or actors. We still use expressions like 'poet laureate', which are reminiscent of this ancient custom. The crown as one of the attributes of a king or emperor certainly dates back to the golden crowns of laurel used by Roman emperors. Possibly diadems are also distantly related to these original laurel crowns.

In contrast with the laurel crown as a symbol of admiration and respect, there was also the crown of thorns – a symbol of disdain and mockery. The crown was made of thorny twigs and was pressed on the head of prisoners or criminals who had been condemned to death.

Most old religious paintings depict a halo. This halo was like an aureola or nimbus and had a very special significance. In fact, only the saints were usually distinguished by this symbol of light and life, shown as a circle of sunlight surrounding the head.

The advent crown also has a religious origin. This crown is made from branches of fir plaited together, and it holds four candles. Advent is the period of four weeks leading up to Christmas, and every week one of the candles is lit. This crown also symbolises a sort of victory, viz., the birth of Christ as the Son of Man.

As stated above, the crown is not only a symbol of triumph; it is an attribute that is sometimes used on joyful occasions and sometimes on melancholy occasions. The triumphant garland round the shoulders of a world champion, the crown of thorns on the head of a convicted criminal, the serious crown of the advent period, the sad wreath on a coffin, the respectful wreath commemorating the victims of war, all represent different aspects of this symbol. Crowns have played a meaningful role in daily life for a long time and will probably continue to do so for many years to come.

1

Make two coils of dough the same length from two similar pieces of dough.

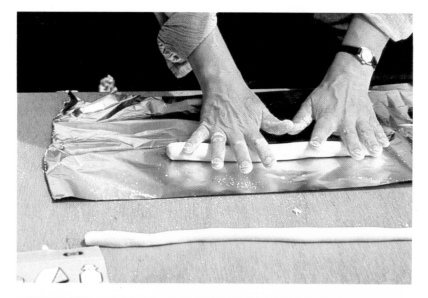

2

Roll out the second coil until it is the same length as the first coil, making sure they are the same length.

3

Twist the two coils together to form a cord.

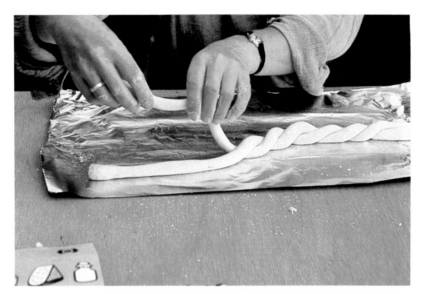

4
Continue twisting the coils together up to the end so that one cord is formed.

5
Make a circle with the cord and join the two ends with water.

6
Check that the circle is perfectly round.

7

You are now ready to start decorating the garland. Fashion a small flower from a piece of dough and prick it with a skewer.

8

Prick the flower onto the garland with the skewer after wetting this spot on the garland.

9

Fashion a leaf and press the veins in the dough with a skewer.

10
Make all the veins of the leaf in this way.

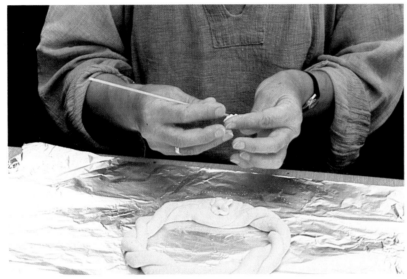

11
Then make more of these leaves.

12
Arrange the flowers and leaves on the garland with the skewer.

13
Add more flowers and leaves. Always make sure you wet the garland first.

14
Continue decorating the garland in this way until the visible ends of the garland have been obscured and there is an attractive cluster.

15
To make a bird, roll a small ball of dough.

16

Model the ball into the shape of a bird.

17

Carefully form the pointed beak by pinching the dough between the thumb and the index finger.

18

Stick the bird onto the garland with some water.

19

Make the wings using the skewer.

The tree of life

The tree of life is a traditional symbol in the mythology and religion of many different cultures. The tree was believed to possess a creative force by many and was regarded as a symbol of the constant renewal of life and was seen in relation to divine forces.

In India the tree was known as the divine mother, the bearer and renewer of life. In Egypt the fruit of the fig tree was known as 'the bread of life', and the Ancient Greeks even identified the tree with a god: the god Dionysius was worshipped in the form of a tree.

Thus on the one hand, the tree was the source and renewer of human life as well as animal and plant life, while on the other hand, the tree was viewed as the symbol of eternal life, of life without death. Presumably the latter interpretation is based on Christianity, and in particular on the biblical story of the tree in the Garden of Eden which gave immortality to the first two people on earth (Genesis 2:9). When they broke the divine command and were sent out of paradise, Adam and Eve also lost their claim to the 'tree of life'.

This interpretation relating to immortality is not only a Christian one, as is revealed by numerous paintings from heathen cultures, which reveal startling similarities with the biblical stories about the tree of life. In the introduction a reference was made to the Mexican custom of making beautiful bread dough sculptures representing the tree of life to honour the dead. Pottery examples of these works can still be found throughout Mexico and Peru, with many different variations.

Babylonian mythology, which dates back even earlier than the ancient Mexican civilisation, contains references to a plant, 'tree of life' or 'herb of life', which had the power to give youth to old men. Another example is the 'apples of Idunu' amongst Germanic tribes, which also had the gift to eternal youth. The Jews and Islamic civilisations also contain pictures which are reminiscent of the tree of life.

Obviously not all the figures and depictions of the tree of life are made from dough or pottery. The same tree of life can also be found in beautiful murals and pen and ink drawings, in artistic cast iron ornaments, decorative wood carvings and intricately embroidered cloths. Because of its symbolic significance, it is usually depicted as a green and leafy tree laden with life-giving fruit.

The fact that the tree still plays a part in our own world as a symbol of strength and life is clear from the custom of planting a tree when a child is born. In Flanders a nut tree or apple tree is planted for a boy and a pear tree for a girl; they both grow in the same way as the children. In Limburg a wedding tree is sometimes planted in the garden in front of the house to symbolise the marriage. The well-known Christmas tree is another version of the philosophy of the tree of life.

The tree of life made in this chapter from dough is a simple example. The two figures represented under the tree can be recognised from the biblical story of Adam and Eve, but the example also shows the tree of life in general as a symbol of new life, personified in the figure of the child next to the woman.

1
Make a soft ball of dough for the top of the tree of life.

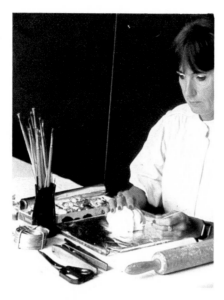

2
Flatten the ball of dough with the fingers.

3
Roll out the dough with a rolling pin. Place a piece of cling film over the dough to prevent it from sticking to the rolling pin.

4
When it has been rolled out, lie the dough on a sheet of aluminium foil.

5
Join a roll of dough to the top of the tree with water: this forms the trunk of the tree.

6
Prick holes in the dough with a skewer to prevent air bubbles or cracks forming when the dough is baked in the oven.

7 Make a long wire hook and press into the dough.

8 Cover the hook completely with pieces of dough. Wet the place where the dough is pressed down.

9 If the tree has dried out, keep it slightly moist with a plant spray.

10 Stick the base, a roll of dough, under the tree with water.

11 Fashion the leaves from small balls of dough and press the veins in with a knife or skewer.

12 First stick the leaves down round the outer edge of the dough, keeping it wet all the time.

13

Stick down the leaves in circles, working from the outer edge of the dough inwards. Arrange the leaves overlapping in tile fashion and stick down with water.

14

The tree of life is now completely covered with leaves.

15

The apples which hang in the tree can also be made from small balls of dough, but it is possible to use beads instead.

16

Use only glass or wooden beads and press them into the dough. Plastic beads might melt when the tree is baked in the oven.

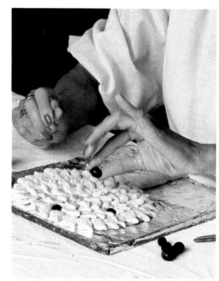

17

For the snake, make a coil of dough of the same thickness all over. Make the head by pressing the end between the fingers.

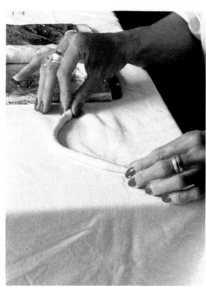

18

Hang the snake vertically in the tree. Wet the place where it is stuck down.

19 Use a small knife or skewer to create the texture of the snake's skin.

20 Use peppercorns for the snake's eyes.

21 Press the two peppercorns down in the snake's head.

22 Stick a slice of dough on either side of the trunk with water as a basis for the figures.

23 Fashion a body from a short roll of dough. Cut the bottom half down the middle with a knife to form the legs, and fashion the feet.

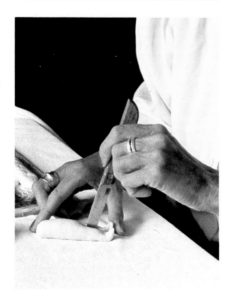

24 Stick the body down on the base next to the trunk with water and stick the head and arms onto the rest of the body.

25

Make the hair using a garlic press, making the hair for the woman slightly longer.

26

Finish off the woman by sticking on the mouth and breasts with water. Prick the eyes with a cocktail stick.

27

Form the body of the man as shown in photograph 23.

28

Stick down the body of the man onto the base on the other side of the trunk with some water, and add the head and arms.

29

Finish off the man with hair, eyes, mouth and sexual organs.

30
Press the small body of the child against the woman, wetting it first. Cut away any part of the base that is still showing.

31
Press the man's nipples and navel with the back of a skewer.

32
Make the head and arms of the child and stick onto the body with water. Cut away the excess dough.

33
Finish off the child with hair, eyes and mouth. Stick down some more leaves under the three figures as a support.

34
The tree of life is finished and can now be carefully moved from the work surface onto the baking tray and into the oven.

35
Bake at a low temperature for about two hours. Raise the temperature of the oven slightly after about an hour and a half. The tree of life is ready when it is hard and a golden yellow colour.

A two-tone squirrel

When you are walking through the woods you can sometimes suddenly be surprised by a beautiful bushy tail flashing up a tree trunk.

You may even wonder whether you really saw a squirrel, because these little reddish brown devils can disappear without trace as suddenly as they appear.

The most striking feature of the squirrel is undoubtedly its wonderful reddish brown bushy tail. The tail is almost as long as the creature itself. Like other rodents that jump from tree to tree or climb up trees, the squirrel needs its six inch tail as a steering device when it swings through the branches, as well as to keep its balance. This enables it to run through the tops of the trees with amazing rapidity and agility. When it has to escape from a predator, it can jump from a great height in the treetops, keeping its balance by spreading its paws and long tail. Like a cat, the squirrel will always land on its feet.

Squirrels are real woodland creatures. Their brown fur is a good camouflage, and with their short paws and balancing tail they are completely adapted to life in the treetops. Their flashing white bellies are only visible from below when they are falling from above, and possibly this serves to frighten off any enemies that might be prowling on the ground.

The squirrel's diet consists mainly of plant matter. It lives in deciduous woodland as well as in pine forests and feeds on seeds in pine cones, acorns and beechnuts. The squirrel's sense of smell is so good that one sniff at a nut will tell it whether the contents are edible.

Everyone is familar with the image of the squirrel with its comical plumed ears and sharp pointed face, sniffing at a beech nut it has found and which it holds firmly between its two front paws. It looks as though it is engaged in a quality control test on the nut.

Squirrels usually store away a proportion of the nuts that were energetically gathered together in the summer. In this way they build up large stores of nuts and seeds which make it possible to get safely through the long winter. If the squirrel's winter supplies are exhausted by spring, it will turn to buds of leaves, eggs, and even young birds. For this reason many other inhabitants of the woods are not as fond of these lively, bushy tailed creatures as most people who imagine squirrels innocently chewing on nuts.

There are even foresters who supply squirrels with seeds and nuts during this period so that they will lose interest in birds' nests and fledglings and the new buds on the trees.

Like so many other mammals, squirrels build their nests in the spring. The expectant mother builds a round nest with twigs and moss, usually high up in the top of a tree. Sometimes she will take over an abandoned magpie's nest for convenience. In most cases the mother will make two bolt holes in the sides of the nest. In case of danger the squirrel can escape an enemy as quick as a flash, and at the same time the openings mean that the squirrel can quickly come to the rescue from any direction when her babies are threatened.

Although squirrels have always been portrayed as very timid creatures in literature, there are always places in the woods or the park where they will not avoid human beings and are glad to be fed.

1
Fashion a ball of dough into an oval body on a board covered with a sheet of aluminium foil.

2
Make a branch from a roll of dough by cutting it slightly open at either end.

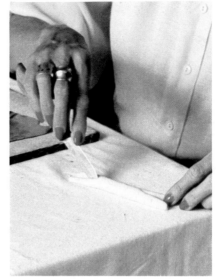

3
Stick the branch to the rest of the body with water.

4
Form the oval head from a ball of dough and stick to the body with water.

5
Stick a small ball of dough on the snout to form the nose. Also form an oval ear from a small ball of dough and pinch to form a point.

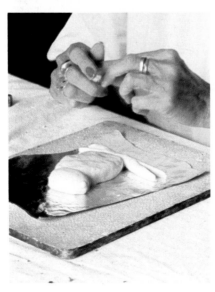

6
Stick the ear onto the head with water. Use a peppercorn for the eye and press roughly into the middle of the head.

7 Finish the snout by pricking a few holes around the nose with a skewer; these are the whiskers.

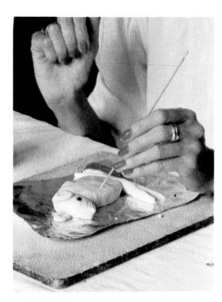

8 You can find the alder cones and acorns in the garden or in the woods.

9 Roll out the lower paw of the squirrel and press the 'hand' shape with a skewer or knife. Stick the paw onto the body with water and press an acorn or alder cone into it.

10 Roll out the upper paw and again press the hand shape with a knife or skewer.

11 Lie the second paw over the alder cone and stick to the body with water.

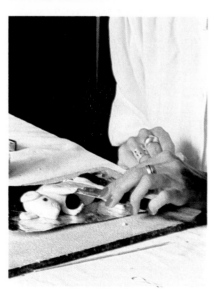

12 Stick the hind paw of the squirrel to the bottom of the body on the branch, wetting the area first.

13
Fashion a hind paw with the thigh.

14
Stick this paw onto the body with water so that the foot is resting on the branch.

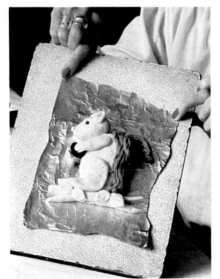

15
For the tail use coloured dough (with cocoa powder) and press through the garlic press.

16
Make long dark brown strands with this dough.

17
The tail can be made with this dark brown dough. Arrange along the back of the squirrel.

18
Finally, stick a wire hook into the body between the head and the tail.

Following like sheep

The sheep, that familiar, placid, woolly, ruminating creature, originated in the Middle East. The nomadic tribes travelled round with their flocks c. 7,000 years B.C. when farming, the growing of crops and animal husbandry began to develop. Before that time the sheep, which is related to the goat and ibex, only lived in the wild and was far less common.

The sheep was very important for the first farmers. The bones were used to make weapons, as well as the skin, the flesh, the milk, and obviously the wool. When it was time to slaughter some animals the healthiest sheep were spared and in this way, either consciously or unconsciously, a better quality sheep was bred.

The wild sheep became a domestic animal and lost many of its original and natural characteristics. Initially sheep had robust horns, sometimes gracefully spiralling, but gradually these horns became smaller and in some breeds they disappeared altogether in the course of time. The creatures themselves have also become smaller over the centuries. The sheep's natural habitat is moorland or other open stretches of land. Strangely they thrive in areas with relatively poor soil and in a damp climate. When large areas of Europe were cleared of their original dense deciduous and evergreen forests to make way for agriculture, and to build roads and towns, sheep could also be kept there. Travelling nomads eventually settled in that part of the world, bringing their sheep with them.

Nowadays the sheep is still a very important creature for its meat, milk and wool. However, sheep are also very useful to farmers because they improve the quality of the grass where they graze. The sheep tirelessly clean the fields and meadows where they graze, even eating the driest thistles with great enthusiasm.

Moreover, it is a well-known fact that sheep play an important role in the conservation of moorland areas. These form an artificial biotope where the combination of animals and plants is determined by factors of climate and soil, and which originated when man cut down the original deciduous woodlands. By grazing sheep on the moorland the ground remains sparsely vegetated, as green plants and shrubs do not have the chance to survive. Heather (Erica and Culluna) thrives. These plants attract bees as well as all sorts of beautiful butterflies. In this way sheep are indirectly responsible for creating recreation areas where thousands of holidaymakers and daytrippers come to enjoy themselves every year.

Although you can no longer imagine the moors without sheep, the number of shepherds has dropped considerably. The image of the shepherd wandering over the moor with his flock, accompanied by his faithful sheepdogs, can still be found in reality, although it is far less common than in the past. Because it is so rare, visitors to the moor find the idea all the more attractive, especially in the spring when the darling little lambs are gambolling around their parents.

1

Roll a soft ball of dough on a wooden board covered with aluminium foil.

2

Press the ball of dough with the fingertips and form an oval body from this.

3

Press a wire hook into the dough from the top. You can also use a paperclip.

4

Prick holes in the body with a skewer to prevent bubbles forming when you bake the sheep.

5

Form the sheep's head from a ball of dough and stick to the body with water, overlapping slightly onto the body.

6

Press a very small ball of dough on the head with a skewer, wetting it first. This is the eye.

7
Use a skewer to scratch the sheep's mouth and nose.

8
Press a small ball of dough flat, make a few lines with a knife and stick on the sheep's head with some water to form the ear.

9
Roll a thin coil of dough.

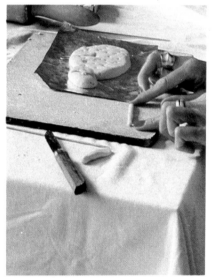

10
Curl this coil over the head around the ear; this is the horn.

11
For the tail, take a long coil of dough, press the end flat and make a few stripes with a knife or stick.

12
Stick the tail to the body with some water.

13

Roll four coils of dough for the legs; make a hoof by cutting the coil open a little way with a knife.

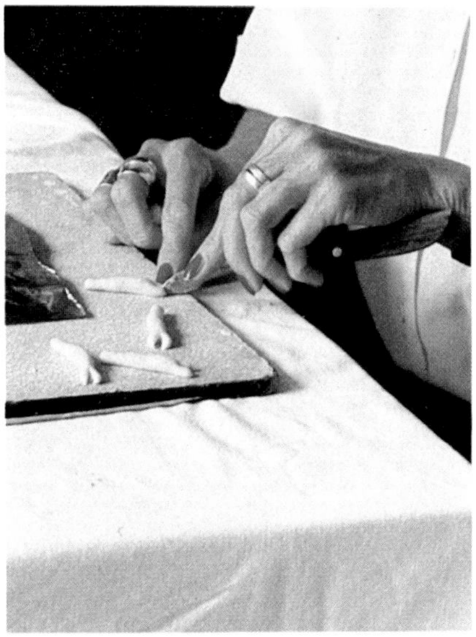

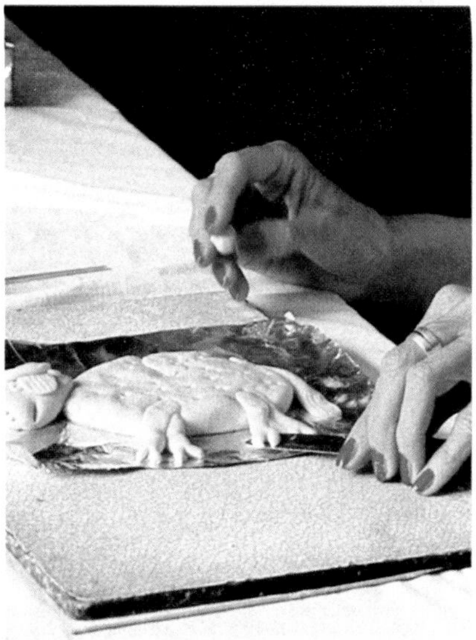

14

Stick the four legs to the body with water, overlapping slightly onto the body.

15

If the dough becomes too dry, keep it moist with the plant spray.

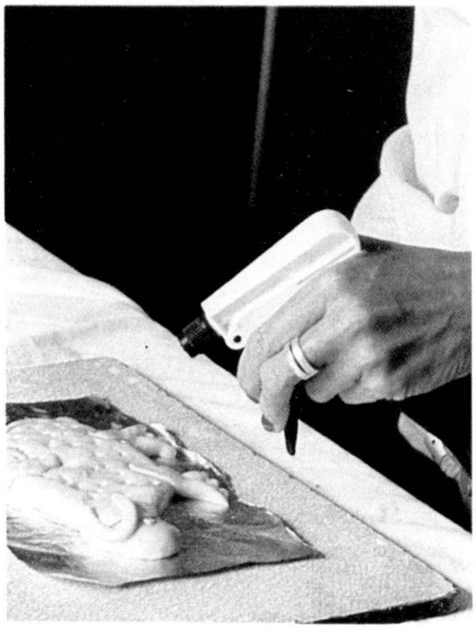

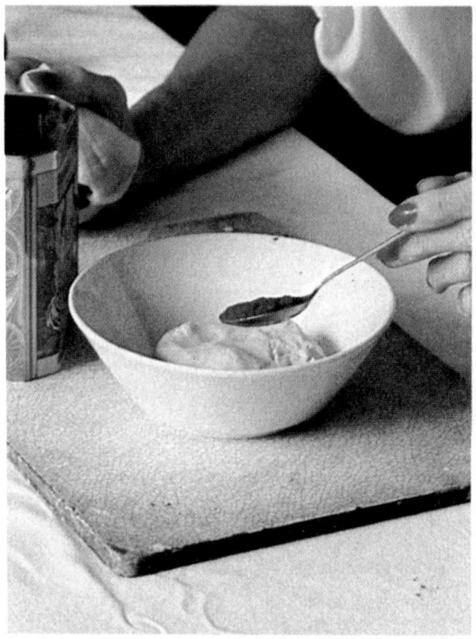

16

Make some coloured dough using cocoa powder (mix thoroughly) for the sheep's fleece.

17

Knead the dough thoroughly until it is an even dark brown colour.

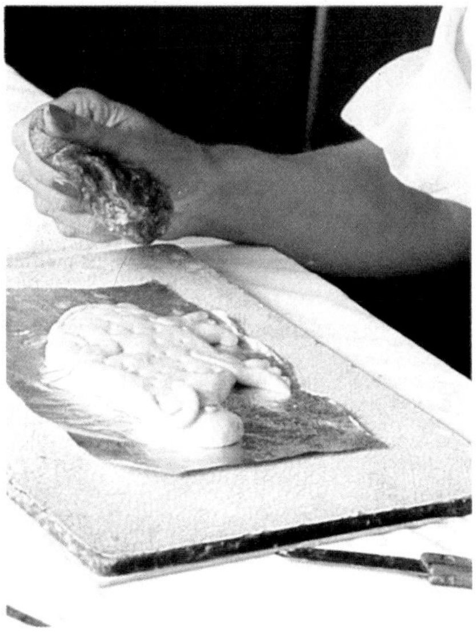

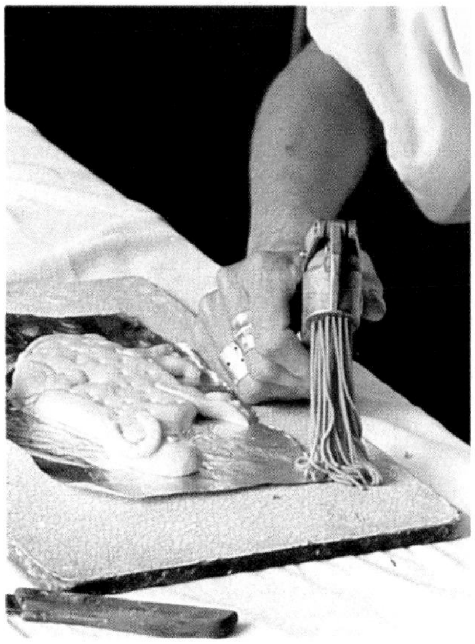

18

Make some long dark brown 'wool' threads with the garlic press.

19
Arrange the strands of brown dough over the sheep's body from the top down.

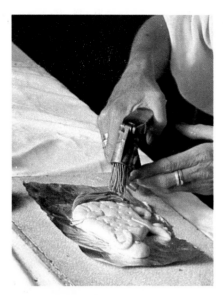

20
Cover the sheep with 'wool' and it is ready to be baked.

21
Put the sheep in a moderately warm oven and bake slowly.

22
A flock of sheep after baking. In these sheep the horns and hoofs have also been made with coloured dough and the eyes have been highlighted with paint.

Bread sculpture presents

It is easy to imagine that you will be so pleased with your figures that you will put them in a place of honour in your home. However, remember that your bread sculptures could also make extremely original presents. You could try to make a number of small figures to decorate your presents; there is no need to follow any set design, so you can let your imagination run riot.

The same applies to small Christmas presents. The little hanging figures in the photograph are made for the Christmas tree, but there is certainly no need to restrict yourself to angels. Small animal figures, garlands and birds also look very attractive in the Christmas tree.

1
Various decorations for the Christmas tree. A special effect can be achieved by sprinkling some glitter in the wet varnish.

2
These Christmas angels are made in the same way as the other little dolls in this book (see p. 29 etc.)

The figures of children made with dough make a lovely present for children or adults. You must put the hook in the dough when you are making the figure so that you can hang it up later. Make the hook from a piece of wire, which you fold into a loop and then twist the ends firmly together. Make sure that the hook is firmly anchored in the figure; the end of the loop should be about half the length of the actual figure.

Another original present to make with dough is a small flower basket, obviously filled with a bunch of colourful flowers, dried flowers, or flowers actually made from dough as well. The basket can be made in all sorts of shapes. You can experiment with all sorts of ideas for presents, for this chapter gives only a few of the endless possibilities.

3 **4**

You can decorate all sorts of objects with this imaginary flower, such as the wrapping for a present, a candle holder, a photograph frame etc.

This decorative flower can always find a place in the home.

5 6

Some holly twigs and red berries on a plain background – this makes a colourful and attractive table decoration.

A decorative flower could be worn as a necklace on a chain.

7
A richly decorated candleholder in which the colours are well matched.

8
A lullabye.

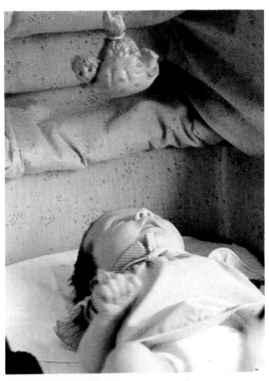

9
A little doll in traditional dress

10
A happy looking barbie doll.

11
A garland in natural colours.

12
A chicken.

13
A plaited basket of flowers.

14
An open basket.

15
The four hearts were made with a pastry cutter. They can be painted in any colours that you like.

16
Decorated with a colourful ribbon, this heart can be used for all sorts of purposes.